BFI FILM CLASSICS

. . . .

Edward Buscombe
SERIES EDITOR

Colin MacCabe and David Meeker
SERIES CONSULTANTS

Cinema is a fragile medium. Many of the great classic films of the past now exist, if at all, in damaged or incomplete prints. Concerned about the deterioration in the physical state of our film heritage, the National Film and Television Archive, a Division of the British Film Institute, has compiled a list of 360 key films in the history of the cinema. The long-term goal of the Archive is to build a collection of perfect showprints of these films, which will then be screened regularly at the Museum of the Moving Image in London in a year-round repertory.

BFI Film Classics is a series of books commissioned to stand alongside these titles. Authors, including film critics and scholars, film-makers, novelists, historians and those distinguished in the arts, have been invited to write on a film of their choice, drawn from the Archive's list. Each volume presents the author's own insights into the chosen film, together with a brief production history and a detailed filmography, notes and bibliography. The numerous illustrations have been specially made from the Archive's own prints.

With new titles published each year, the BFI Film Classics series will rapidly grow into an authoritative and highly readable guide to the great films of world cinema.

Could scarcely be improved upon ... informative, intelligent, jargon-free companions.
The Observer

Cannily but elegantly packaged BFI Classics will make for a neat addition to the most discerning shelves.
New Statesman & Society

THE BIG SLEEP

. . . .

David Thomson

BFI PUBLISHING

First published in 1997 by the
BRITISH FILM INSTITUTE
21 Stephen Street, London W1P 2LN

The British Film Institute exists
to promote appreciation, enjoyment, protection and
development of moving image culture in and throughout the
whole of the United Kingdom.
Its activities include the National Film and
Television Archive; the National Film Theatre;
the Museum of the Moving Image;
the London Film Festival; the production and
distribution of film and video; funding and support for
regional activities; Library and Information Services;
Stills, Posters and Designs; Research;
Publishing and Education; and the monthly
Sight and Sound magazine.

British Library Cataloguing-in-Publication Data
A catalogue record for this book is available from the British Library

ISBN 0–85170–632–0

Designed by
Andrew Barron & Collis Clements Associates

Typesetting by
D R Bungay Associates, Burghfield, Berks.

Printed in Great Britain

CONTENTS

For Richard and Mary Corliss

ACKNOWLEDGMENTS
. . . .

I am grateful for the assistance of several archives: to Bob Gitt of the University of California Los Angeles film archive, for information on the recently discovered 'early' version of *The Big Sleep*; to Jim D'Arc and the Howard Hawks archive at Brigham Young University, Provo, Utah; to Ned Comstock and Bill Whittington of the Warner Brothers collection at the University of Southern California, Los Angeles; to Tino Balio and Special Collections at the University of Wisconsin, Madison, Wisconsin; and to Stanley Brown and the Irving Thalberg script collection at Baker Library, Dartmouth College, Hanover, New Hampshire.

I was helped a great deal by talks with the late Lady 'Slim' Keith. Maurice Rapf, Todd McCarthy and Patrick McGilligan gave good advice. My first viewing of *The Big Sleep* – and of other Hawks films – was enriched by the company and talk of Kieran Hickey. Which reminds me to honour the late Richard Roud, who programmed the first Hawks season at the National Film Theatre in London in 1961.

I have also benefited from Hawks talk with Andrew Sarris and Molly Haskell, Richard Jameson and Kathleen Murphy, and Richard and Mary Corliss.

And I thank Rob White and BFI Publishing for asking me to write.

8 Outside the Realito hide-out (publicity still)

'THE BIG SLEEP'

· ·

For decades now, since a Saturday in 1961 when I saw it three times in a row, coming out of one screening at the National Film Theatre's original Hawks season and joining the queue for the next (as if the movie were a ride on a sensational fairground entertainment), I've regarded Howard Hawks' *The Big Sleep* as my favourite film. Or, if not quite that, then the most entertaining, the most rich, confident and comfortable. It's a picture you want to curl up in, like Bogart and Bacall in their tiny car, just looking at each other and practising kissing, while music and fate build up outside like a thunderstorm. It has always seemed to me, somehow, the happiest of films, so relaxed and yet so controlled: seeing it offers the chance of a rapture like that of being in love.

And I can hardly separate my good spirits from the steady spectacle – at full or three-quarters length – of the drably dressed Bogart carrying all before him: standing up to the heat of General Sternwood's greenhouse; rallying at the net with Bacall; pushing Joe Brody in a circle until the creep cracks; plugging Canino; kissing Mrs Rutledge, and just generally looking so damn good and being so wry that you feel better about everything. It's a dark world, and nearly every composition offers the shape of claustrophobia, if you want to feel gloomy. But Bogart handles himself and the space as deftly as Jo DiMaggio running left field. The space is like his shadow, or familiar.

Now here I am, years later, having volunteered to write something useful about the film, and for another great celebration of Hawks. Will there be new kids who have never seen it before, and be as delighted as I was? I hope so. But, still, as I try to be useful, I have to notice how odd this happiness is, and how disguised a form it takes. Maybe that's the first hint of Hawks' unique perversity or indirectness. Ask him to make a film about happiness and he'd have gone fishing, or got drunk. But give him a story about more murders than anyone can keep up with, or explain, and somehow he made a paradise. Maybe he needed a cover, some way of seeming tough, cool and superior, if he was ever going to do happiness.

After all, in lots of ways *The Big Sleep* looks and feels like Fritz Lang, a man whose 'happy' scenes are about as encouraging as sweet breath in someone preparing to torture you. It is an interior film, without sunlight, fresh air or real nature. Though its compositions are not as intense, not as filled with convergent psychic toothache as Lang's, still they are formal, orderly, enclosing and dictated by the specially designed sets. That any Hawks film feels more open or optimistic than any Lang picture isn't merely in their different attitudes to composition. It's more that Hawks is always looking at people, their gestures, their antics, their personality, with an eternally sad respect and fondness; whereas Lang sees shapes, against which the human figures are on the rack and pressured. Hawks' approach was so anecdotal and so ready for surprise – but still he composed his shots like a man who shared Lang's basic notion that there was no escaping fate. After all, *The Big Sleep* looks and sometimes feels like a film noir, which – clearly – is a mistaken or much less than adequate labelling of the movie.

Nevertheless, if you step back from the pleasure or the happiness, or whatever you elect to call it, you have to begin to see the ways in which Hawks has denied himself things that Raymond Chandler, say, appreciated. There is not one moment in the movie of *The Big Sleep* when proceedings get out into the potent open air of southern California or when the film sees the kind of thing Chandler noticed in his first sentence in 1939, the way in which 'It was about eleven o'clock in the

'It does rain in the movie, but this is rain laid down on studio streets by sprinkler systems'

morning, mid October, with the sun not shining and a look of hard wet rain in the clearness of the foothills.'

It does rain in the movie, but this is the rain laid down on studio streets by sprinkler systems, the puddles placed like beauty spots, the lights arranged so that rain looks like the night's negligée. Indeed, there are studious efforts to play fair by nature in the movie. When Marlowe goes bookstore hunting, there is an appealing air of some Los Angeles street, and yet it has no sky, no real threat of wildness, and so Marlowe strolls and drolls around, as elegant as Astaire. And when he goes up to Geiger's house in the hills, there is a charming masquerade of hilliness, with a garden, inclines, trees and damp night air. So much care has been taken to avoid just going out and finding some pretty, sinister nook in those Hollywood hills that could be Laverne Terrace, Geiger's place, and the kind of address you have to check out carefully to make sure it never existed in L.A. Looked at closely, the elaborate, craftsmanly exterior set is every bit as arranged as what Marlowe finds inside the Laverne Terrace cottage. And then later, much later, when Marlowe goes down to Realito – which, if you think about it, is a name to tease detectives and scholars – we get a lovely atmosphere of road, mist and a wayside garage. But it's all a set, a moody gesture towards the little town Chandler dreamed up in orange grove country:

> The groves thinned out and dropped away to the south and the road climbed and it was cold and to the north the black foothills crouched closer and sent a bitter wind whipping down their flanks. Then faintly out of the dark two yellow vapor lights glowed high up in the air and a neon sign between them said: 'Welcome to Realito.'

Chandler had mixed feelings about L.A. and southern California, even if nowadays he is used as a spokesman for nostalgia's golden age. After all, it was reading Chandler as much as anything that reminded a real Angeleno, Robert Towne, of the places, the airs and fragrances of his childhood, so that in *Chinatown* and that film's mid-to-late 1930s (before Marlowe's October morning) Jake Gittes has a nose and an eye for landscape and the faint, metallic tang of what might be water (or iniquity). Gittes is a good deal of a cynic: he feels more modern than Marlowe, even though he predates him. Gittes is far readier than Marlowe to compromise, to be pushed around by fate. But he has sounder roots than Marlowe: he has a palpable history and failures already; he falls in love and he is stirred by the sheer wicked wonder of how Los Angeles has been contrived out of the desert. He might wince a little at Robert Towne's romanticism, but he has been coloured by it:

> And if at five in the afternoon you happened to find yourself down by Union Station during a Santa Ana, you could feel the warm dry itch across your skin, look down the tracks to the mountains and sky and the pastels of lavender, salmon, and blue the color of painting from old tile-topped motels long since blown to rubble – you could still see the city [Carey] McWilliams and Chandler wrote about and I remembered in those last moments before sunset.

That's Towne in an essay on how he came to write *Chinatown*, and it's testament to a legacy from Chandler that has affected screenwriters, writers in the age of movies, and many Los Angelenos. This is the notion that the place, its weather, its light and its nearness to earthquake, fire and landslide are all begging metaphors for a city that has always enjoyed hovering between real and realito. The city has changed, and not much for the better: so much of the old Spanish flavour has gone, the air has become more toxic, and that pleasant hovering is now more evidently unstable, or crazy. But Angeleno detectives relate to the place, and what it means. Gittes gazes into pools of water. The Marlowe of Altman's *The Long Goodbye* appreciates the beach at Malibu. And even in 1996's far more modest *Mulholland Falls*, the four fedora'd L.A.P.D. men – the partners – marvel at the huge, abrupt, shockingly beautiful crater in Nevada where the government is experimenting with vaporising cities. In L.A., you see, there has always been a brief, hallucinatory interval between the air and the light and the solid things.

After all, in Chandler's *The Big Sleep*, when Marlowe's had his round with General Sternwood and then another with Vivian Regan, not to mention the early routine with Carmen and Norris, he takes stock and places the Sternwood mansion (3765 Alta Brea Crescent – precise as a clue, but off the maps) in space and history:

> I stood on the step breathing my cigarette smoke and looking down a succession of terraces with flowerbeds and trimmed trees

to the high iron fence with gilt spears that hemmed in the estate. A winding driveway dropped down between retaining walls to the open iron gates. Beyond the fence the hill sloped for several miles. On this lower level faint and far off I could just barely see some of the old wooden derricks of the oilfield from which the Sternwoods had made their money. Most of the field was public park now, cleaned up and donated to the city by General Sternwood. But a little of it was still producing in groups of wells pumping five or six barrels a day. The Sternwoods, having moved up the hill, could no longer smell the stale sump water or the oil, but they could still look out of their front windows and see what had made them rich. If they wanted to. I didn't suppose they would want to.

So much of Chandler's shy, bitter morality rests in those two afterthought sentences. They let us know that Chandler feels we're on a fault zone here, that many successful Angelenos need to learn a way of overlooking their own past and back story. Whereas Hawks' Marlowe is never anywhere near shy, uncertain or ethically perturbed. He takes a certain amount of wickedness for granted – his favoured line in dry, deadpan jokes relies on that great force of human frailty. He has no plan for eradicating it, and no fear that it could corrupt him. So Hawks never lets his Marlowe have moments of reflection (or that intimate voice-over), where he looks down from the hills and feels the measure of the past. This Marlowe, after all, is flawless, superb and utterly self-sufficient, save for one thing. He wants someone to talk to, the way a comic needs a straight man (or woman). It's rather like Walter in *His Girl Friday*, who hardly notices murder, death sentences or human beings in his rapt search for a scoop, but who is getting edgier and as sharp as a hunter wondering if he might lose Hildy, might even end up alone – and silent.

So Hawks' Philip Marlowe doesn't really come to the Sternwood mansion to earn his $25 a day, plus expenses, or to hold back the remorseless pressure of crime and malignancy in L.A. He wants a little fun, and some good talk. He's ready to let life be empty or absurd, so long as it's not boring. The routine of existence, the plainness, the ordinariness – these things are to be eclipsed by comic routines, lines, scenes, and indelible meetings. Hawks did meetings as if his life depended on it – and so it did, I think, because if there hadn't always been meetings and new doors ready to open he'd have had to get into something more profound

1 4   Marlowe overhears the last words of Harry Jones ('one of the greatest things in the book and the m

and terrifying. Like the real squalor of the Sternwood sisters, the creeping entropy of L.A. and the disaster of lives like that of Harry Jones.

Harry (Elisha Cook) is one of the greatest things in the book and the movie, and it's interesting to consider how far he is someone who isn't quite tall, insolent, eloquent or magnificent enough to be Marlowe. After all, they look a little alike, and they wear similar clothes. What does $25 a day get you for wardrobe? Marlowe's suits are as dark as noir, charcoal and grey, impersonal. There's no more character in his white shirts and plain ties. Nothing fancy, nothing to notice. It is costume suited to the world of shadow and a kind of monastic solitude. We get a good look at it in Sternwood's hothouse as the jacket comes off, the tie is loosened, and Marlowe grows circles of sweat on his white shirt.

Which is an opportunity to remind ourselves that Chandler's Marlowe is very differently garbed. I break this gently to you purists of the movie, but in the book Marlowe wears a powder-blue suit! A dark blue shirt! And black socks with dark blue clocks on them! Why, if Bogart's Marlowe is somewhere between an urban priest and the angel of death, Chandler's suddenly seems fruity, a fop, a dandy, and a startlingly needy, neurotic guy. This could be the one who goes into Geiger's bookstore with an affected lisp! Whereas Hawks' shamus is a saint, or a Satan, a paragon, someone beyond weakness or need of expressive costume. Face it, this man is so unreal he *might* end up in perfect happiness!

. . . .

Raymond Chandler's *The Big Sleep* was published in February 1939. The author was fifty, and at last moving from being a story writer, often for pulp and mystery magazines. He lived in Los Angeles with a wife eighteen years his senior, and he was less than pleased with his world. He was a worrier with uneasy feelings about writing and Los Angeles. But his first novel was a big step forward: the Knopf hardback sold 10,000 copies (very good), and a shrewd, favourable review in the *Los Angeles Times* reckoned that Humphrey Bogart would be ideal casting for Mr Chandler's private eye, Philip Marlowe – that was ahead of the movies of *High Sierra* and *The Maltese Falcon*, pictures that altered and warmed the actor's screen identity.

Chandler's Marlowe was a character far beyond what was expected of pulp fiction detectives. He had a very deft way with a funny line, so that nowadays – once L.A. and the tricky plots have passed into the realm of 'nostalgia' – we can feel the comic writer in Chandler, yearning to find a suitable form. Marlowe can tease the tawny sexpot, Carmen Sternwood, tell her his name is Doghouse Reilly, catch her as she collapses in his standing lap, and tell the butler, Norris, 'You ought to wean her. She looks old enough' – a terrific punchline that ends the first chapter and makes the reader hungry for more of Marlowe's laconic humour.

He is thirty-three (thirty-eight in the film), a college graduate, 'and can still speak English if there's any demand for it'. He's unmarried, and apparently a little too independent for an earlier job with the D.A.'s department. There's a very plain office for his work, but no secretary. He lives quietly, playing chess with himself, at the Hobart Arms in a room that is 'all I had in the way of a home'. He doesn't like it when he gets home one night to find Carmen naked and very ready in his bed. He knows she's dangerous and unstable. He has 'professional pride', too: he's working for her father. And finally it gets on his nerves that she has intruded on his privacy – that room: 'In it was everything that was mine, that had any association for me, any past, anything that took the place of a family. Not much; a few books, pictures, radio, chessmen, old letters, stuff like that.' (You can see how the first-person narration can hardly exclude self-pity – whereas in the movie Bogart simply moves and exists with the force of uncomplaining, unexplaining presence.)

This man has no family, no private life, just a kind of immaculate loneliness that is odd in a man who says such funny things. Because usually those guys long to get a laugh, or a response.

Howard Hawks was not quite as witty as Marlowe, but he liked to say smart things in a casual way that left people laughing. Not that he joined the laughter. No, he stayed quiet and aloof; he could be flat-out icy so as not to laugh. This was his way of holding on to a necessary solitude – a kind of space in which he wanted to be seen, and in which he saw himself.

Less than a year before *The Big Sleep* was published, Hawks was at the Clover Club, the best gambling establishment in Hollywood, up above Sunset. He was forty-two but he looked older, or more distinguished, because his always tailored clothes, and his handsome impassive face, were topped off by prematurely silver-grey hair. That night, at the Clover Club, he was taken with Nancy Gross, a tall, twenty-year-old blonde, born in Salinas and raised in Pacific Grove, near

Carmel. She was a knock-out, with brains: 'I thought it was more important,' she said, 'to have an intelligence that showed, a humour that never failed, and a healthy interest in men.' Hawks asked her if she wanted to be in movies, and she told him no. It was an answer he had never heard before – new, challenging and faintly disdainful.

Hawks was as classy in Hollywood as Walter Wanger – and both men had a trace of fraud as a result. Though born in Indiana and raised in Pasadena, Hawks had been sent to a very proper prep school (Phillips Exeter) and to the Ivy League (Cornell). We must wait for Todd McCarthy's biography to be sure of the details, but Hawks in his offhand way did suggest an uncommon background of wealth and distinction. He had fine, clipped manners to go with his expensive clothes. He had been in the Army Air Service; he had flown planes and driven racing cars – he said. Or, rather, he let it be concluded.

Seen from an admiring distance (that space he preferred), Hawks was easily 'placed' as a special man of the world. When *Movie* magazine made its tribute to Hawks, in 1962, it said of him:

> He makes the very best adventure films because he is at one with his heroes... For Hawks, who drove racing cars for a living and built aeroplanes before he was twenty, men prove themselves through mastery of their own actions. In any of his adventure films, we know that the hero must, for his own satisfaction, complete what he has taken upon himself.

That happy self-sufficiency still has currency, and there is no doubting the charm of a kind of lonely, half-twisted professional code in films like *Red River*, *Rio Bravo*, *Only Angels Have Wings* and even *His Girl Friday*, where the adventure for Walter consists of keeping Hildy off balance so that he always tops her in their battle of talk and manoeuvre. You can see just how twisted, and even cruel, that can be in the way Walter may always need to be divorced by Hildy so that he can once again prove the mastery of his own actions, and others' minds, by winning her back. Better that game, Hawks seems to say, than the risk of stagnation in explored marriage. Where's the fun in that?

As he got into his elegant pursuit of Nancy Gross, and she declared herself more and less than a would-be movie girl who'd let herself be bedded for a test or a scene, he introduced her to his two children. For Hawks was married, to Athole Shearer, the sister of Norma Shearer. Not that that had ever slowed him in the standard Hollywood sport of the powerful – fucking around, all in the search for a new girl who clicked on screen. And anyway, Athole wasn't quite 'right', not really normal. She had fits of depression that amounted to illness. A philandering husband never helps that condition, but still the word in town was that Athole was a little crazy and that she had earned her reputation the honest way.

And so in the year that *The Big Sleep* was published Hawks was pondering how to divorce Athole tastefully – after all, a certified spouse couldn't actually be detached – and marry Nancy, or 'Slim', as he and so many others called her. Athole took out a divorce suit – or was it taken on her behalf, by her mother, Edith? It was conceded that Athole was 'terribly afflicted', yet Hawks was given most of the blame for his 'cruel and inhuman treatment'. Afterwards Athole, with $1000 a month from Hawks, was put in a rest home in La Jolla, and Hawks was given custody of Peter Ward, Athole's child by her first marriage, as well as that of the two children Athole had given him. Nancy stuck it out for the several years of waiting, so much younger than Hawks, so easily regarded as

Athole and Howard Hawks

sexual plunder for him. But she loved him and his terrific air of mastery – over scripts and life: 'So I hung in there for dear life. A lot of it was tedious and discouraging, and in many ways undignified – as any woman who's been the girlfriend of a married man will understand.'

Those awkward years might make a fine movie – even one by Hawks in which the plot is played for laughs just to show you how close you are to tragedy or gruesomeness. Athole would be an especially delicate part. But as *Bringing Up Baby* had shown, Hawks was a wonder at telling a love story that was scrambling to keep out of the swamps of dementia. Susan in that film, however much fun she is, is splendidly, bravely and blindly afflicted. But her world never rebukes or confines her.

Hawks had just made *Bringing Up Baby* when he met Slim. He also had *Dawn Patrol*, *Scarface*, *Twentieth Century* and *The Crowd Roars* to his credit. But he was an oddball, an independent, a man who avoided going under long-term contract through the 30s. Indeed, he had walked away from, or been fired for insubordination from, two big pictures – *Viva Villa!* and *Come and Get It* – just because he was difficult or proud; aloof or constitutionally averse to being produced. *Come and Get It* was a particular humiliation, for Hawks had shot nearly all of the picture and because he had gone out on a limb to abandon Goldwyn's actress and use Frances Farmer instead, one of his 'discoveries' and 'the best actress I ever worked with'. That was in 1936, when Farmer was twenty-four, looked like Slim, and had something of the same stunning directness: 'She was probably one of the cleanest, simplest, hardest-working persons I ever knew. She came a couple of times to my boat wearing her sweat-shirt and her dungarees and carrying a tooth-brush in her pocket. She had no phoniness about her at all.'[1] That dream! Of course, Farmer was a little afflicted herself; she might have done Athole very well – if she could have kept the pain under control. I'm stressing this rather queasy side to life in order to make clear just how intense or uncompromised a love story *The Big Sleep* will be; and how far its wishful core of love, or romance, defies the movie's elaborate noir trappings. It is all very well to look at *The Big Sleep* as just a thing up there on its screen, a series of black-and-white spasms – and it is gloriously artificial, self-contained and apart from reality. But just as film commentary has learned to temper the hero-worshipping auteurism that would see Hawks as the master player of that game, so a widening consideration of studio practice and ideology needs to take in yet another area: the private lives of those who made the film. For in the dream factory, we should never forget how often a movie – hacked out in days and weeks of hard, practical work – was also the daydream and the fantasy of those who made it.

. . . .

Hawks and Nancy Gross were married in December 1941, four days after Pearl Harbor. There's a way of regarding their partnership as a golden, if brief, union, of two very handsome, clever people mutually drawn to the enchantment of style and grace under pressure. They knew Hemingway, and at times they both behaved like a couple in one of his books – the Colonel, say, and his adoring Italian girl in *Across the River and into the Trees*, that very precise, matter-of-fact, this-is-how-you-shoot-a-gun-and-drink-the-cold-grappa-and-love-your-girl-in-a-gondola fantasy. They were their own characters, and they sometimes called each other 'Slim' and 'Steve'. They talked a lot, and they talked in character. He loved her all the better in that she had great lines – mock sultry, flirtatious and witty – lines like 'You do know how to whistle, don't you?' This was the repartee of twin beauties who reckoned on being in the sack in twenty minutes. If they could stay in character.

It's easier to measure the gap between self and 'character' with Hawks than it is with Slim. In part, that's because we have her autobiography where she talks about him, and the way he made or presented himself. Whereas Hawks, in his several interviews, never reflects on the act; he *is* the character. Your writer knew Slim a little, forty years later, when she was plump but otherwise smart still, fun, brave (she was not well and not well off) and thoroughly stylish. She still admired Hawks, from the ideal distance (he was dead by then), and regarded his oddities, and his habit of lying, as an author might muse over a character still being written. For in marriage she learned several defects or qualifying conditions about her 'Steve'. He was very cold. He was a chronic gambler. He was a dedicated, poker-faced fantasist. And he was a liar.

In the years since *Movie*'s celebration of Hawks – the editorial of which ended, 'Everything that can be said in presenting Hawks boils down to one statement: here is a man' – I've found ample evidence to support Slim's charges so that, by now, it's maybe easier to sigh over Hawks and say, 'Just like a man.' He wasn't a sweetheart. But he wanted

22 Nancy 'Slim' Hawks (Howard Hawks collection, Brigham Young University)

to think well of himself, and he wanted somehow always to be the hero in his own, unwinding movie. In life as in his pictures, dignity and self-respect were first principles. I don't disparage that weakness: it seems to me a way of getting along in Hollywood, and even for most of us in the age of movies, raised as we are on these superb, complete, constitutional fantasies. We are all Walter Mittys from time to time, in the secrecy that fantasy must have. But Hawks was a day-dreamer who broadcast his dreams, and Slim was there with him, an instrument in the fancy. She could not miss the way his own script faltered:

> Howard built such a fantasy life about himself that he came to believe it was true. He never thought I would square the fact with the fiction, but I did, simply by hearing him repeat the same stories to fresh audiences. Each time, the material was different – he would completely rewrite his script.
>
> It's not that Howard was a liar because he wanted to best you or steal from you. He just had a terrible time with the truth. His lying was a psychopathic quirk. He dreamt when he was awake and he slept a totally dreamless sleep.

You begin to see what *The Big Sleep* could mean to Hawks – as a title. Now, I don't mean to say that Slim was undivided, or that she was so bracingly free from phoniness every moment of the day and night. She had had to work out a way of justifying what happened to Athole. She had done her best to be 'mother' to Athole's kids (though they were not that much younger than she was). She had had to ignore Howard's ceaseless affairs and flirts – rather as in *The Big Sleep* Vivian has to rise above Marlowe's 'helpless' schmoozing with every cigarette girl in sight (and Hawks did have a way of seeding his films with wisecracking knockouts who have a quick scene, a shining, and then vanish).

Not that Slim was necessarily immune to dalliance. She had a reckless streak, and she was only about the most beautiful woman anyone had ever seen, with smarts that needed no finishing. Indeed, she had gone from her convent school not to college, but to San Simeon and the Furnace Creek Inn (in Death Valley), where she quickly attracted the attention of vacationing movie people. Nor am I confident about believing that she never wanted to be *in* pictures, despite what she told Hawks. For not only was she handsome; she carried herself like a model – and not just for clothes: she was an example for behaviour, and for how a young woman swam with older sharks. She talked back, told them off, made fun of them, and all in a way that enslaved them further. She had Hemingway, Gable and Gary Cooper among her 'swains': Leland Hayward would be her next husband.

Hawks and Slim would have a daughter, born while *The Big Sleep* was being done, Kitty Steven Hawks. By then the marriage was foundering, and it was no help that Hawks was not around much during the pregnancy or the childbirth. But Slim, and the extra financial burden of Athole, did coincide with what may be Hawks' greatest years – *Only Angels Have Wings*, *His Girl Friday*, *Sergeant York* (his biggest hit), *Ball of Fire*, *Air Force*, *To Have and Have Not*, *The Big Sleep* and *Red River* (for which Slim persuaded Montgomery Clift to take a chance on a Western). And the crest of that period, the deepest pitch of Hawks' waking dream, is when the romance of 'Steve' and 'Slim' transcended all the awkwardness of life. Which begins with their shared discovery of Betty Bacal (the second 'l' came later).

Betty's mother had left Romania as an infant. In New York, at City College, she met and married William Perske. Betty was born in 1924, and grew up looking like nothing else on earth. I mean, how does one describe that young woman who could look like a Jewish teenager, a Eurasian doll, a Slav earth mother and the smoke that gets in your eyes – and all that before Hawks got hold of her? Add to that the allegation that she was only seventeen, and you can see what a wide-open country America was then.

When she was sixteen, Betty did some classes at the American Academy of Dramatic Arts. She dated Kirk Douglas a little, and got an old coat of her father's to give to the penurious young actor. When Kirk joined the Navy, he wrote her fond letters, but nothing had happened. She began to do modelling work, and she got a part in a play, *Franklin Street*, written by Arthur Sheekman and Ruth and Augustus Goetz, and directed by George S. Kaufman.

At the age of eighteen she got an introduction to *Harper's Bazaar*, and it was for that magazine, in January 1943, with Diana Vreeland directing her, that she 'posed in a blue suit with an off-the-face hat, standing before a window with "American Red Cross Blood Donor Service" lettered on it'. It was a Louise Dahl-Wolfe picture and it made the cover of the February issue. You can see the figure of a nurse through the frosted glass of the Blood Donor window, and Bacall is leaning against the edge of the glass, her unsmiling face tipped over to one side. She does look eighteen, and yet she looks thirty-five, too, with a hint of twice that. The look on her face is lethal. There's a low light on her face and her wide mouth. It's noir lighting, no matter how close we are to medical help. Maybe it's just me, but I feel she's the vampire who waylays you on your way to give blood. It's a picture that suggests vocations and urges above and beyond the war effort.

In California, Slim saw the magazine: Hollywood wives have time for much reading. She seems to have been following Bacall, who had been used in earlier, less prominent pictures. This very arresting pose settled the matter. Slim was appealed to: 'She was certainly my taste in beauty – scrubbed clean, healthy, shining and golden. And there was definitely a bit of the panther about her.'

This was February 1943: the all-male *Air Force* was a month away from opening. Slim had had time to learn how easily Hawks was led astray by a pretty face. But she was still, also, professionally interested in his 'type', and so she showed him the magazine and said something like 'What about her?' Try as we may to elevate the role of directors, it is

How closely was Bacall's look and persona (here in *To Have and Have Not*) modelled after Slim's?

impossible to get the faintly sinister connoisseurship of the meat market out of movie-making. And the admirers of film's final beauty would do well to bear it in mind.

Hawks was never dumb about faces, and for 1943 this one was riveting – so long as the face could talk the way Slim talked. The director called Charlie Feldman, his agent and then his partner, and got Feldman to find out who the girl was. In New York, Miss Bacall got approaches from the Selznick office, from Columbia and from Charlie Feldman. He asked her to come to the coast and do a test: she would be on $50 a week until such time as a contract – personal to Mr Howard Hawks – was settled. That was how it would be. Miss Bacall had round-trip travel, a hotel in L.A. and $50 a week. She left in April. Years later, in interview, Hawks said there had been a mistake. He *had* seen the picture, and been interested, but his secretary jumped the gun and initiated the contact. 'All I wanted,' said the elderly Hawks, in charge and cool again, 'was to find out her background, whether she'd studied, whether she'd played any scenes, what she'd done. Instead of that, she arrived.'

What's a director to do? He worked with Bacall. He did tests of her, and played around with her hair. The tests are fascinating. For, if they put up her hair or curled it too much, Bacall looked not just ordinary but a little gauche and forbidding. There was something humourless in her face – she wasn't a natural smiler. Her own voice was high and pinched. So Hawks told her to go out into the Hollywood hills and practise speaking with a low voice. She found a desolate stretch of Mulholland Drive and read aloud from *The Robe* to the jackrabbits.

Bit by bit, Hawks put her together: the voice, the hair falling down one side of her hard face, the droop of her mouth, the shy stare in her eyes, and that air of a depraved nineteen. She worked hard at it, without quite knowing what 'it' was. After all, it was something Hawks had glimpsed, or intuited, and he wasn't a sharer. Then, one evening, he got into a talk with her. They had been to a party and it was his chore to drive her home – this is Hawks remembering: 'Can't you get a ride yourself,' he said, 'so that I can get tight and not have to drive you back?'

'I don't do too well with men,' she told him.

'What do you do, are you nice to 'em?'

'Nice as I can be.'

'Why don't you try to insult them?'

So a week passed, and she came sauntering over to him, looking pleased with herself.

'Well, I got a ride home,' she said.

'What happened?'

'Oh, I insulted the man.'

'What'd you say?'

'I asked him where he got his tie. He said, "What do you want to know that for?" And I said, "So I can tell people not to go there."'

Which is an awfully pretty, cool way to remember it. Slim Hawks saw it differently. She said that Hawks deliberately copied her own teasing, kidding way with men, just as he duplicated a lot of her clothes – tweed suits and berets, long, soft dresses with big, boxy shoulders – and named the character that was emerging Slim. 'Once he hired Betty, he suddenly became very interested in everything I had to say. Now he listened to me as if I were speaking lines created by the screenwriters Jules Furthman and William Faulkner. In his eagerness, Howard would sometimes show his cards and directly ask me what I'd say in a certain situation. Dutifully, I'd answer the question. The next thing I knew, Furthman and Faulkner were running it through their typewriter.'

According to Slim, Furthman said she should have shared screen credit. Hawks didn't offer that, but he made his wife co-partner in the contract by which they owned the services of the woman who was getting to be Lauren Bacall.

The actress was having a good time – she liked Slim, especially, and her only real problem with Hawks, she said, was having to ignore his anti-Semitic remarks. He was of that old-fashioned Hollywood – WASP, Ivy League, men's men – who reckoned that too many Jews were bad for the business, rowdy, graceless and uncool (though he had been Irving Thalberg's brother-in-law, and part of the Thalberg crowd). The creature who was gradually becoming his dream shut up and never told him she was Jewish. But she wondered what it was all for – if Hawks knew how she ought to stand and look at people, what was the story?

Then, early in 1944, he said that maybe he could put her in the film he was going to do of Hemingway's *To Have and Have Not* – already set up as a Bogart picture. Hawks and Feldman had bought the screen rights to the novel, and they had traded them to Warner Brothers. He gave Bacall a love scene from the script – with the whistling bit – and she rehearsed it with John Ridgely:

John Ridgely would sit in a chair opposite Howard's desk, and I had to sit in his lap and kiss him. I was self-conscious and very nervous. Howard told me how to sit and where – made me do the whole thing while he watched. Kissing is fairly intimate – to do it with a man you hardly know and your mentor is watching and your future hanging in the balance is enough to put fear into the heart of a fairly experienced actor – to a novice like myself it was utterly terrifying. And I desperately wanted to be good for Howard – I couldn't bear to have him feel he'd signed a dud.[2]

Never forget that moviegoing is a voyeur's delight (and torture) or that the first voyeur is the director – the one who prefers to watch, and has to school the actress's rapture. Later on, after things had gone very cool between Hawks and Bacall – no matter that being cool was her thing – and after he had sold her outright to Warners, by which time she and Bogart were crazy over each other, someone whispered in her ear that maybe she should have been a little 'nicer' to Howard, in the way of putting out for him. After all, he was making her, wasn't he? What had transpired was a man's elaborate coaxing of his dream into life, so that at the magic moment, when he sent the stand-in Ridgely away and called in the star – that sad, edgy, alcoholic Bogart, a man with a toupee! – why Bogart won the girl and stole the dream. *To Have and Have Not*. You have always to see with Howard Hawks how the great romance and adventure are so close to frustration and black comedy – You Can't Sleep Here.

. . . .

What of Bogart? *To Have and Have Not* is one of the climaxes in his great romance, that legend in which the tough, wry hero at last gets his just reward – an insolent, 19-year-old sexpot with blow jobs lurking behind her sultry gaze. 'Bogey and Bacall' – it passes for history in our addled regard for show business. But love and sex in real life are often so much more messy than in movies, and so much closer to compromise.

In 1943 Humphrey Bogart was forty-four, and a success at last: the breakthrough of *High Sierra* and *The Maltese Falcon* had been established by a silly picture no one expected much from, *Casablanca* (maybe the first women's picture made for men), dementedly elevated by the way its opening coincided with the real relief of another north

African city, named Casablanca. As if America or Warner Brothers understood that actual place!

Just as we need to remember that Bogart came to mean 'Bogie' (Bogie or Bogey? Bacall uses 'Bogie' and Louise Brooks prefers 'Bogey') only after his death, so it's vital to an understanding of Bogart's gloom on screen that he had been around over a decade without achieving unequivocal stardom, or being sexy. Though he worked hard through the 30s, it was often in supporting roles and invariably as a villain – there was scant opening for Bogart in his pictures to think well of himself. There were those, like Louise Brooks, who saw him as a rather repressed, naggingly inward guy from the upper-middle classes, pained at being a hoodlum and driven to anxiety, booze, meanness and insecurity. I know this goes against the grain, but there is no reason for taking it for granted that the insouciant Bogart of *The Big Sleep* ever felt so assured in life – no matter the longing.

Casablanca had changed things for Bogart. But he'd heard the role might have been George Raft's first, and he recollected that Ida Lupino had been given top billing on *High Sierra*. On *Manpower*, Bogart had been further rattled by stories that Raft didn't want to act with him. By

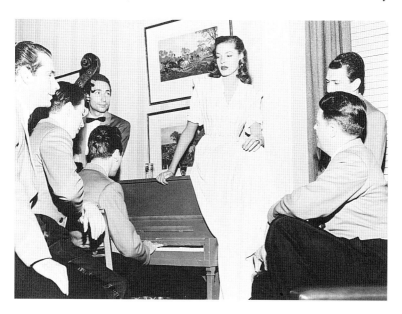

Singing in Eddie Mars' place (publicity still)

then Bogart was on the third of his marriages – all of them to actresses. His current wife, Mayo Methot, was a fellow-drinker, a trouble-maker, and someone whose scenes he had come to fear. Yet at the outset of their relationship, in the mid-30s, 'she set fire to him. Those passions – envy, hatred, and violence, which were essential to the Bogey character, which had been simmering beneath his failure for so many years – she brought to a boil, blowing the lid off all his inhibitions forever.'[3]

But Mayo's rescue act had turned sour, leaving the violence and the drinking that aggravated it. At which point Bogart got his first chance ever to play a love story. Admit that that's what *To Have and Have Not* is (it *is* a Douglas Sirk kind of title), and you see the sort of attitude Hawks brought to Hemingway – even if the two men had been shooting buddies together, up in Idaho. It was probably on such an expedition that Hawks had thought to buy the rights to the book; Howard Hughes had got them originally (in 1937) for $10,000. Hawks and Charlie Feldman had to bid up to $97,000 for them. Warner Brothers then bought the rights from them for $108,000 plus 20 per cent of the gross (up to $3 million).

That was the sort of deal Hawks was famous for: he had a great knack at moving in on a studio, imposing his terms; and then acting like a free agent and his own producer. It was a neat way of persuading himself that he was his own master. But Hawks also saw *To Have and Have Not* as a spin-off of *Casablanca*: the two films share Bogart and the idea of a resolute freelance who elects to join the war, and an intense, enclosed setting where guys and dolls hang out, waiting for the action but ready for music. It was a very romantic view of the war, and one that required a 'love interest'. Hemingway's *To Have and Have Not* is so much grimmer and less escapist. The novel's Harry Morgan has a wife, an older, dowdier woman, back home. He also knows a life of true poverty and unmistakable danger. He dies. Whereas the movie of *To Have and Have Not* is a glorious fantasy in which the solitary 'Steve' gets the 'Slim' of his dreams, slinky, witty and first seen holding up a limp doorway the way a 19-year-old can bring stamina to a middle-aged hard-on.

Bogart and Bacall fell in love, in sex, or in fantasy – very likely a mix of the three, for how are actors supposed to keep the threads of so many dreams separate? Bacall was young, new and ambitious; she was also – thanks to Hawks, Slim and cameraman Sid Hickox – giving off a look and a breathy sound that still seem like one of the most startling debuts. Bogart was romanced by this panther, and all he had to do was sit there, be relaxed and grin as he played a deft, fearless adventurer who handles everything. It says something about Hawks' vanity that he didn't see that coup coming – or maybe it was just that his conjuring up of a fantasy was more absorbing than actual interaction. He was maybe a touch too cool to show his neediness.

Whereas Bogart yielded to the thought of another rescue. On set, he and Bacall had the same sense of humour, though there were people who'd worked with Bogart who'd never seen him laugh. He was looking after the newcomer, too, in the way of a veteran who begins to realise the kid is stealing the picture. After three weeks of work he came into her dressing room at the end of the day and just kissed her. He asked her for her phone number, and she gave it. An affair developed, and Hawks could not miss that. He became her stern, rather grumpy proprietor. He told Bacall she was a naughty girl, that she was responding to Bogart more than to his direction. What's a girl in love to do, asked Slim — Howard had called her in as co-proprietor – hardly unaware of ironies in the situation.

What was Bogart to do? Hawks warned Bacall that this was only a passing fling for the actor. That was how Hollywood operated; it was his own practice. So Bogart would fuck her and then drop her. The fantasy wasn't meant to last longer than the shooting schedule or 97 minutes on screen. So Hawks was miffed, yet ecstatic, for he was too good a director, too much into sultriness and suggestion, to miss what he was getting on screen. Once again, he was in the most delicate voyeuristic state – he was watching. He told Bacall that if she didn't pull herself together he'd likely sell her contract. 'And the funny thing is,' Hawks mused years later, in his best old-man storyteller mode, 'that Bogey fell in love with the character she played, so she had to keep playing it the rest of her life.'[4]

Maybe – and what an interesting subject for a movie, albeit of the kind they seldom risk. *To Have and Have Not* was released in January 1945, and it was a hit, no matter that it remains very difficult to define the film precisely: is it a war picture, an adventure, a love story, a comedy? All of those, at least. Well before its opening, Warner Brothers had conceded that it would be a success. They tried to forget their earlier campaign to dissuade Hawks from using Bacall. Not only was he securely his own producer at the studio, he had made a star.

3 2   A scene 'undreamed of by Chandler', a mating ritual between Marlowe and Vivian

What else could those two do, the studio asked. It happened that Hawks and Feldman already owned the rights to Chandler's *The Big Sleep*. They sold them to Warners for $20,000 in October 1944. In due course Hawks (and Slim) would also sell their contract on Ms Bacall to the studio. In the meantime, Bogart could be Marlowe … and Bacall? Well, Eddie Mars' wife, Mona, is the character in the book who saves Marlowe's life. Carmen Sternwood has the best, sexiest scenes with him. And there was also Vivian, Mrs Regan in the book, wife to the Irish adventurer who has vanished. Or maybe they'd fashion something new for 'the girl', just so long as she was in there somehow.

In real life, Bogart was striving to live up to his young rescuer. He wrote her notes and they had lovely trysts in parked cars. He would leave Mayo, that maker of drunken scenes. He did; he moved into the Beverly Wilshire. Then, in tears, he confessed that he had gone back because Mayo was sick and a danger to herself. The divorce came slowly and painfully, and it needed the second blast of fantasy's shotgun, *The Big Sleep*, which was made with Bogart in agony, in tears and turmoil.

. . . .

Hawks liked to imply the extent of his own authority and terrain by talking of scripts as the necessary, rather broad and hasty instruments that provoked inspired improvisation on the set. There's no reason to doubt the way he worked. Time and again over the years, Hawks would start a day's work less by rehearsing a scene than by 'kicking it around': the actors would do a read-through and Hawks would encourage the notion that this was all really rather dull and how the hell could they make some 'fun' out of it? It was an offshoot of that way of working that, at some moment amid the mayhem of *The Big Sleep*, more to make conversation than in search of meaning, Bogart asked who had done one of the killings in the story. No one had the answer, not Hawks nor Jules Furthman, his favoured 'on-set' writer. So they asked William Faulkner and Leigh Brackett – no dice. Then they called Chandler (never far from the production), and he didn't know either. Such details were no loss, and no real problem, so long as the requisite kind of fun was being generated.

Faulkner and Brackett – the one a drinking companion and a prestigious literary name; the other someone who had initially been mistaken for a guy – had hacked out a first working script. Allegedly they did this in eight days, with Faulkner taking some scenes and Brackett others. Then Hawks and Furthman presided over the spontaneity of the set, enormously aided by actors who could learn new lines – and often complex dialogue scenes – in the hour or so while the lights were being set. For if Hawks improvised first, what the actors said on camera was both precise and controlled. From which you might easily deduce that in filming Chandler's *The Big Sleep* Hawks and his team just took hold of the original and guided it, artfully yet idiosyncratically, into another medium with all the aplomb of people pouring wine from a barrel into a glass.

But in the process the nature of the fluid altered. Just as the severity of Hemingway's male world in *To Have and Have Not* had been dispelled by 'Slim', the hysterically sophisticated, invulnerable and yet available young thing in tweeds and satin (Hawks liked to suggest the feel of his women, and while his camera style was famously 'detached', he was wild about textures), so Marlowe's solitariness in Chandler's book and his jaundiced view of the world are overcome by his attraction to Vivian. Indeed, there is little doubt at the end of the movie that these two are together for all time, wreathed in shared cigarette smoke, in the experience of having come through danger together, and in that very Hawksian mutual admiration of 'looking good' in a two-shot. They are the real, living images to go with the silhouetted figures over the credits (though the woman there, I think, is not Bacall). So many American films end with people 'together', without the nature of marriage being posed or explored. But here was a movie for which the marketing people at Warners would have been ashamed of themselves if they hadn't locked into the public awareness that Bogart and Bacall had themselves been married on 21 May 1945 (over a year before *The Big Sleep* opened).

That closure is magnificent and moody. The cigarettes hark back to the introduction this couple had on screen in *To Have and Have Not*. They gaze at each other as police sirens well up in the background, to be joined by Max Steiner's music. There will be questions to be answered, there is Carmen to be handled, and the General to be told. But – to be as practical as divorce lawyers – it looks as if the $25-a-day private detective is going to marry Vivian and be, so to speak, the General's heir. Why not? We have felt the respect between Marlowe and Sternwood. Why shouldn't the General have a decent drinker and talker for his last days? And Marlowe can inherit Norris, that ideal butler. You can even see a future with Marlowe, Vivian and Norris as a detective trio – that could be a TV series, couldn't it?

3 6   The hidden camera in Geiger's house used to frame Carmen

Above all, though, there is the way Bogart and Bacall look at each other, a rapport deeper than that of Marlowe and Vivian. This is an enduring portrait of love and companionship (not to forget sexual intimacy); it is a classic moment in film and celebrity history, and a resounding last shot, the lovely light at the end of the tunnel.

Whereas in the book Marlowe has a Vivian who is sexy, greedy, cold, manipulative, dishonest and very ruthless. She tries to buy him off, with $15,000, to forget about Carmen having killed Rusty Regan (Vivian's husband in the book) and being likely to kill again. She's just a nasty rich bitch who only ever dallies with Marlowe to control him. He turns on her with nothing less than loathing, in a long, nearly self-pitying speech about the integrity of $25 a day – 'and maybe just a little to protect what little pride a broken and sick old man has left in his blood, in the thought that his blood is not poison, and that although his two little girls are a trifle wild, as many nice girls are these days, they are not perverts or killers. And that makes me a son of a bitch.'

Vivian goes silent and contrite, but there is never any hope for her and Marlowe. She promises to take care of Carmen; he gives her three days' grace. As for Marlowe, he just wants out. He drives away, holding to his solitude and the determined moral righteousness that goes with it, and is so wayward as to pick socks with clocks on them and that garish powder-blue suit:

> What did it matter where you lay once you were dead? In a dirty sump or in a marble tower on top of a high hill? You were dead, you were sleeping the big sleep, you were not bothered by things like that. Oil and water were the same as wind and air to you. You just slept the big sleep, not caring about the nastiness of how you died or where you fell. Me, I was part of the nastiness now. Far more a part of it than Rusty Regan was. But the old man didn't have to be. He could lie quiet in his canopied bed, with his bloodless hands folded on the sheet, waiting. His heart was a brief, uncertain murmur. His thoughts were as gray as ashes. And in a little while he too, like Rusty Regan, would be sleeping the big sleep.

This Marlowe seems almost to dream of his own death, as withered and depleted, but as honourable, as General Sternwood. That is the bond of duty (patron-client) that holds him, and next to it the two Sternwood girls are treacherous sirens, threats to a certain code of male understanding. Marlowe goes to a bar. He takes a couple of drinks: 'They didn't do me any good. All they did was make me think of Silver-Wig, and I never saw her again.'

'Silver-Wig' is Mona Mars, who heeded the argument for decency and gave Marlowe a chance in his final confrontation with Canino. In the book Mona is alone, and her act of rescue is grudging (for she realises how far she is going against her husband). But in the movie Vivian is there with Mona, and it is she who takes the decisive action and stands by her man. This is part of the essential transformation of the adaptation. Even at their first meeting, the audacious exchange of sweaty detective and martini-cool Vivian (a scene closely based on the book), the film contrives to discover a level of sexual innuendo and hostile attraction not really grasped by Chandler.

The hinge, I think, is the way the movie adds to the book's scene Marlowe's repeated reminder to this lady of the house that her father had offered him a drink. He interrupts her and she interrupts herself with the savage 'Help yourself!', whereupon he loses his thirst (it *would* be his third drink before noon) and tweaks her interest. How deftly he has got under her skin and how surely his sweat prickles her smooth surface. The bickering talk has nothing to do with a 'case' he is on, and everything to do with their growing and mutual attraction. But this is no sentimental fondness. For Hawks there was no romantic or sexual interaction without the comedy of cross-purposes, misunderstanding or traded barbs. In other words, the love – that thing – must never be owned up to in the obvious, uncool way. How well that works on screen, yet how dismaying it might be in life. (You will recall that coldness was one of the things Slim Hawks lamented in her husband.)

The earlier conversation between Marlowe and the General is very fine, very literary (no matter how sick he is, this General can still think to speak of champagne as 'cold as Valley Forge'), and well located in a jungle of plants where Marlowe proves himself even as he is wiped out by the humidity. Charles Waldron is so delectable and fiery as Sternwood that we hope he may reappear – he is also so strong, so wise, so eloquent that it is not quite plausible that he is as ill as he claims. But it is Marlowe's meeting with Vivian that sets the emotional tone and the area of play for the rest of the movie. (It starts us thinking that 'the big sleep' can only be the sated peace of lovers, too tired, at last, to talk any more.)

The second Marlowe–Vivian match is brief but very suggestive. (It was an addition to the book; and, as we shall see, an afterthought for the film.) Marlowe returns to the Sternwood mansion bearing a Carmen still 'out' from the Geiger house. Norris is all understanding. The General is asleep (didn't he say he hardly sleeps?). But then Vivian comes floating down a corridor – rather like Cocteau's Belle – in a white silk robe that mimics the languid splash of her hair. She opts to behave as if Marlowe has been responsible for Carmen's state – this is surely just provocative – and he responds with a mocking tirade about how yes, of course, this treatment is part of the detectives' manual. This allows her to flare with anger. Marlowe grabs her by the shoulders and as they ponder rape or rebuke there is thunder and lightning outside so that her face seems to flex in the strobing like a panther's snarl. 'You go too far, Marlowe,' she hisses.

That phony line is really a kindness, a lob begging for the smash, so Marlowe simply turns away and walks towards the camera (with Vivian silkily posed in the background) on the line, 'Those are harsh words to throw at a man, especially when he's walking out of your bedroom.' By now the 'case', or the 'job', has become just a pretext for the swordplay of insolent wooing. The Carmen dropped on her own plush bed was a kind of love offering, and, gently, we begin to feel that Marlowe and Vivian have sex, talk and a task in common – helping to hold the family in place.

The next meeting between eye and eyeful is the scene where she's waiting for him in his office (can she get inside him, too, already?). This is taken from the novel, but radically energised for the movie. She is in hound's-tooth tweeds and a beret, full of sauce and nerve, and so edgily tactile that she gets an itch in the soft skin above her knee. Scratch, he tells her (it is another interruption to the main threat of talk), and she goes at herself with a nearly masturbatory zeal. As so often with Hawks, tiny gestures or phrases can loom like zeppelins of subtext. There is a half-hearted notion that Vivian has come to his office to find out where he is on the investigation, even to mislead him, but the look on her face is flat-out randy. She just wanted to see him again. Scratch for him. He *is* under her skin.

The exuberant mating ritual finds expression in one of Hawks' greatest scenes – undreamed of by Chandler – in which she calls the police, he takes over, and the phone goes back and forth between them, a shared game and their clearest impersonation of 'family'. Notice, too,

40   General Sternwood: 'I seem to exist largely on heat, like a new-born spider'

how as this joke builds each one of them takes a cue without prompting; the game is in their secret nature. They have found kinship.

She grins at him. Bacall had a grin that nothing else in her set, serious face prepared us for. It was a kid's grin, yet lewd, as wicked and filthy as one-of-the-boys.

'You like to play games, don't you?' she says caressingly. It is the realisation that all the insolence and banter are a vein of masked fondness.

'Uh-huh,' he says – does anyone in a Hawks film (except Ralph Bellamy) ever admit to being in love? (Wait and see.) Asked why, this Marlowe opts for circumlocution: 'I think I'm beginning to like another of the Sternwoods.' And she admits she likes that, like someone who has just had a remarkable foot massage, or was it cunnilingus? In the aura of indirection, after all, anything can mean something else: indeed, it has to, in order that elusiveness can make a magic dance to surpass the commonplace. It is possibility in American movies, and moviegoing, that excuses the dullness of life. God help us.

Many commentators have reflected over the years on the density, and the nearly lyrical impossibility, of the plot in *The Big Sleep*. It is that impossibility that nurtures the possibility I was talking about: but that formula isn't just a play on words, it's the formulation of an elegant, macabre dead end. Some people say that Hawks is making fun of plot itself – which is fair enough. And he recalled what he learned on the film about throwing out causation and a traceable line. But we know now that there was once, about three-quarters of the way through, a lengthy, ponderous scene in which Marlowe explained to the cops what had happened. The scene didn't play; it was so much at odds with the 'fun' scenes. So Hawks dropped the explanation – and the picture soared free.

But real chaos, disorder, unsettles audiences, and Hawks the easygoing modernist never wanted to risk that. That's why I stress the needs and the pressure of the love story – and our wanting it to build – sustaining the narrative in its confusion. So long as Marlowe keeps moving with assurance, and talking in perfect, funny sentences, the disorder is bearable. And so, when Marlowe goes to visit Joe Brody or Agnes, the reasonable questions of why or who cares can be set aside because he is actually pursuing Vivian. So she must be there too – yet she is not involved in that scene in the book.

In the movie, however, she flagrantly invites Marlowe's suspicions. He is in his office at night when she calls: no news, she says, no one's called. He puts the phone down and twigs. No one in a movie calls to say no news. She is diverting him; she is going to see Joe Brody. So he's there outside the building waiting for her to pull up, and then after a suitable pause he's up the stairs behind her. Joe lets him in. (Joe, by the way, is as brittle and shifty as old crackers in Louis Jean Heydt's performance. Hawks relished working with such crafty pros in small parts: they are the best defence against boredom.)

Marlowe sees the pointed toes of Agnes behind the curtain (Marlowe and Agnes are one of the movie's funniest subtexts – the nagging marriage), and after she has emerged he wonders why Mrs Rutledge shouldn't come out, too. We are in the realm of French farce here, of course, no matter that death will buzz at the door soon. But Bacall's Vivian appears – in another very smart outfit – both mortified and fulfilled, or as haughty as someone doing the tango. She gives Marlowe a baleful, pierced glance, as if to say, you found me. They are true to each other in their trickery.

It's not long before Brody is dead, after opening one door too many. Marlowe chases the killer, Carol Lundgren – don't ask why Lundgren killed Brody – takes him back to Geiger's house and, so to speak, settles

With Agnes in Joe Brody's apartment

the case. Bernie Ohls comes in and a state of understanding is reached: Brody killed Geiger, and Lundgren killed Brody. And then comes another meeting between Marlowe and Vivian. It is, famously, the scene that was done later, somewhat at the urging of Charlie Feldman, who felt that the already cut picture needed another powerful shot of Bogart and Bacall, preferably with the two of them talking in a sly, dirty way.

There's more still to the circumstances behind the scene, I suspect, and I'll return to them later. But, granted that it was done much later – around the turn of the year, in fact – this scene is a kind of comic reappraisal of the whole film, and even Hawks' own belated realisation of what he had been doing. The scene is set in a crowded bar – an airy place – and the piano is playing 'I Guess I'll Have to Change My Plan' as Bacall comes in wearing a jacket as shiny as rain-slicked streets. She takes the waiting Marlowe to a table, tries to pay him off and make sure his mind is moving away from the case. 'What do you do when you're not working?' she asks with the husky, athletic appetite of a panther that has never worked a day in her life. The talk turns to horse-racing and who's in the saddle, and it is as dirty as we choose to hear it. Bacall looks like someone breathless from lapping up cream, while Bogart has the jaunty air of a flattered sultan. Then he snaps shut on her and wonders why she's trying to sugar him so, and why all this sultry chat to shake him free of the case. The case! As if anyone at this point could give a coherent explanation of what that is, or muster a conscientious concern.

In fact, we know now, thanks to the discovery of a prior version of the film, that this horse-sense scene was used to replace the comprehensive, if monotonous, explanation of the case that Marlowe had offered to Ohls and his superior in the first cut of the movie. Dated April 1945, that early version probably played to troops in the Pacific, and it was previewed at home – without great success. The lesson of 'Don't explain, don't complain' (essentially Hawksian) came to the aid of the movie and so plot was wilfully, deliberately forsaken so that 'fun' could be pursued. If the film moved forward smoothly, maybe there was no need for narrative logic. The decision seems obvious now, and it surely releases *The Big Sleep* from archaic rules, but had there been so clear-cut a decision in Hollywood before this?

There's no denying, or escaping, the serene momentum of the picture, its slippery ease. There isn't a scene that doesn't play. The mounting sexual tension between the leads is heady, close to comic, yet

The 'horse-sense scene' shot belatedly to replace the explanation scene which was unliked by the film's first, military audience

The cut explanation scene

very romantic, even if the prolonged double meanings of the horse-talk run a risk of being precious. The steady supply of new characters, or even bits, is life-enhancing: you feel the way Hawks cultivated those bits, if only to kid himself away from worrying about the fragile whole.

But the whole *is* ridiculous, and a commentary fifty years later cannot simply ignore that, or make nifty jokes about it. For movies do have, or posit the chance of, a whole identity: *Red River*, *Rio Bravo*, *Bringing Up Baby* and *His Girl Friday* do have entirely coherent and developed plots about which we care and wonder. Those films are dramas; *The Big Sleep* is something else, a something we still need to puzzle over, for it is both radical and decadent as it relates to the history of the narrative movie.

The deliberate decadence, or parodistic thrust, is much in evidence in the next meeting between Marlowe and Vivian. He has gone to Eddie Mars' place. The question 'why?' would be more obvious if the action there wasn't so cute. He catches the eye of a cigarette girl as easily as a suit picking up fluff. And this pert brunette comes up to him with the word that Mars can see him now as he's attending to Vivian and a kind of glee club singing a collective song – and Bacall here is doing her own singing, as well as finding time to eye the cigarette girl's pleasing body and give Marlowe the high sign. It's a gorgeous exchange, superbly timed and cut and typical of Hawks' ability to get the spatial-emotional reality of a room in just a few shots. That said, it also aids and abets the sultan's dream that life is a harem in which wife number 1 is a merry connoisseur of the other girls.

Why is Vivian performing at the club? (Or are we to think that in 1945 L.A. places like the Clover Club encouraged impromptu singsongs in their customers?) My best answer is that this whole sequence is a performance meant to divert Marlowe's eye. For after he talks with Mars (we'll pass that), he goes out to the roulette table where a Vivian suddenly more resolute than the songstress is beating Eddie for $28,000.

She then asks Marlowe to take her home. He goes out to the car park and spies the thug getting ready to hold her up. So when she appears, in a three-quarter length fur, Marlowe is there to dispatch the hold-up man with one punch and take Mrs Rutledge and the bag to his car. They drive against a travelling projection that could be the rougher part of the Mojave Desert. Until he stops the car and turns to her: she has all along been lying back, half reclining, that thick-lipped Eurasian face swathed in hair and fur (there is at least a hint of sisterhood with Faye Dunaway in *Chinatown* – though being *her* sister was no joke).

There is an intense, rapturous close-up of Bacall in her seat (in a style not much given to soupy close-ups), until Bogart's head juts into the frame to kiss her. 'I like that,' she says, and Steiner's enchanting, very poignant theme comes up – did it manage to sound nostalgic even in 1946? 'I'd like more… That's even better.'

I hope I have by now established several reasons for regarding this moment a little ruefully. Yet I have to admit, fifty years after the movie, after dozens of viewings and much reflection, that I cannot muster anything close to respectable disillusion. The Steiner music, I know, as music goes, is … well, if not quite trashy, movie music, a trick. But it moves me. (My wife, just passing as I played the scene over, stopped to say, 'That music is so good.' It gets you.)

Nor can I shrug off a once youthful, now sadder sense of desire for Bacall herself, to say nothing of this wash of fur, hair, light and lip gloss on the screen. I have known trysts in cars at night (with my wife) when nothing happened more than kissing, and I know that my own romantic life has been affected by the scene and others like it. Not that it was ever done better. So no doubt, irony or maturity yet impairs the adolescent dream that it would be great to kiss such a woman in a parked car and feel that eternity was your spectator.

. . . .

That kissing ends. Kissing's very nice, Marlowe says after he's had his fill, but still Vivian is seeking to hoodwink him. And so the duel goes on. Marlowe is beaten up in the back alley. Harry Jones comes into the story and makes his gulping exit. The mood surely darkens with the appearance of his killer, Canino. There's an air in the last twenty minutes or so of 'fun' being set aside and noir drawn in, like a shroud. The entire Realito episode is gloomy with danger, and there is sadistic aplomb in the way Canino lets ball bearings spill from his hand just after he has slugged Marlowe.

Then Marlowe comes to, and he's tied up and handcuffed, with an open wound on his jaw. Mrs Eddie Mars is there – she's been hiding out in Realito, which was probably as easy as getting Madonna to go incognito. Marlowe rides her, taunts her about Eddie until she tosses liquor in his open wound. And then Marlowe is left with Vivian again.

Vivian takes Eddie for $28,000

Marlowe: 'I don't like people who play games'

No, she's not there in the book. Don't bother to ask why she's in Realito, too – though you might wonder why so few admirers of the movie ask that same question. Of course, she unties him, with another kiss first, the more sensual because he is tied up, and then she sets up Canino for him out in the yard. Then the two of them go to the Geiger house to trap Eddie Mars, and Marlowe makes Eddie walk out of the house first into the hail of fire that was meant for himself. So, at the very end, it's Marlowe and Vivian together, the sirens and the music – you know this bit – two beauties in profile, turned slightly to look at the future. But together. The camera tilts down to the ashtray and the two cigarettes left there at the start of the picture.

I grieve over Eddie Mars still, and not just because John Ridgely does such a good, cool job in the part – and, after all, he helped teach Bacall to kiss for the camera. But what the hell has Eddie done to deserve all this? I know people familiar with the film who never quite register the admission in that final scene that it was Carmen who killed Sean Regan (because he didn't fall for her). All Eddie has done is help Vivian shield Carmen. Sure, along the way this has led to Harry Jones' death – but that was Canino, who plainly kills out of habit. Of course, it is preposterous that Eddie would need to or bother to shield Carmen. And since Vivian – who is by now established as our heroine – is ready to put the unstable Carmen in a home, why wasn't she smart enough to do so earlier? What has all the fuss been about? In the book, of course, Eddie doesn't die. Marlowe walks out on Vivian telling her to get Carmen confined, or else.

Which brings us to Carmen, a neglected figure in film commentary. You may recall that I raised the question about which role Bacall would play in the movie. This seemed proper in that Mona Mars is plainly still on Marlowe's mind at the end of the book, while Carmen is probably the most indelible woman in the novel. But Carmen is the killer, and out of her mind. Moreover, she is also – in her two big scenes in the book – stark naked, which is the kind of set-up that gets movie interest.

When Marlowe first goes to Geiger's house, Carmen is sitting in a high-backed teakwood chair in the pose of an Egyptian goddess. 'She seemed to be unconscious, but she didn't have the pose of unconsciousness. She looked as if, in her mind, she was doing something very important and making a fine job of it. Out of her mouth came a tinny chuckling noise which didn't change her expression or even move her lips.' She is wearing jade earrings, and nothing else. Her body,

Marlowe notes (the eye is a trained observer), is 'beautiful ... small, lithe, compact, firm, rounded. Her skin in the lamplight had the shimmering luster of a pearl.'

Marlowe adds that this body meant nothing to him – she was just a dope, drugged out of her mind. Then later on, after the charade at the Mars club, and after Vivian has kissed him in the car ('Hold me close, you beast,' she said), Marlowe goes back to his own room and realises that 'Something was wrong.' There's someone in the room, in his bed. It's Carmen. 'Then she took her left hand from under her head and took hold of the covers, paused dramatically, and swept them aside. She was undressed all right. She lay there on the bed in the lamplight, as naked and glistening as a pearl.'

The offer is refused. He tells her to get dressed and go home. A pale version of this scene occurs in the movie, one in which Carmen is sitting there, fully dressed, and is easily sent packing. In the book she calls Marlowe a filthy name – one that Chandler won't repeat. But he can't stand her there, tainting his place. Carmen goes away but Marlowe is left with a loathing that still reads mysteriously and more neurotically than Bogart or Hawks could ever have conveyed:

I went back to the bed and looked down at it. The imprint of her head was still in the pillow, of her small corrupt body still on the sheets.

I put my empty glass down and tore the bed to pieces savagely.

At first glance, it's easy to see Hawks dispensing with that scene. After all, in the real movie, in its version of the scene, Hawks has Carmen ask Marlowe (referring to Peter Pan): 'Is he as cute as you are?'

'Nobody is,' Marlowe tells her. And, despite his cocky irony, the film never undermines that assessment. Hawks' Marlowe gets beaten up in an alley once. You could argue that he's helpless to save Harry Jones – and, near the end, he tries to pretend that this has rattled him. But Marlowe is otherwise ahead of the game, always having the last witty remark, solving the infernal case and ending up, as it were, in sole possession. Nor is there a hint of weakness in his armour, much less the torture exposed in ripping that bed to pieces. Did that Marlowe lust after the pearl, or is he appalled that such corruption can exist? Whatever the answer, Hawks' Marlowe would never reveal those shakes – least of all to himself.

Carmen and Joe

Carmen in Marlowe's apartment: a scene much expurgated in comparison with
Chandler's original

Yet as anyone reads the book, Carmen is more arresting than Vivian. The older sister on the page, with her great legs and her kissability, is what the General says of her in the film – 'spoilt, exacting, smart, ruthless'. In other words, she's more pulled together than Carmen, who is Raymond Chandler's and 1939's version of a nymphomaniac. I stress this because I suspect that Chandler was a faithful, timid man who'd never met a nymphomaniac. In the book, it is Carmen who appears first and who has that insolent way of talking – 'Tall, aren't you?' she says to Marlowe. Carmen is also dangerous and sexy. Did it ever occur to anyone to make the two sisters one, and to have Marlowe caught up with, half smitten by and trying to protect and save a girl who … proves to be the real killer? That might have made the story more coherent and urgent, but it would have meant playing Marlowe as more of a sap, someone who could be suckered and taken in. Notice, too, how that plot solution leads the film more surely towards the noir dread of an unreliable woman. After all, it's got a hint of *Double Indemnity*, *Angel Face* or even *Out of the Past*, in which the hero is led to perdition by a two-faced woman.

So it says something about Hawks' personality (and fantasies) that he built Vivian into a partner Marlowe will finally describe as 'wonderful', as opposed to Carmen. But the closer you look at the film, and what we know about its making, the more clouded that decision seems.

In her autobiography, Lauren Bacall makes it clear that she and Hawks were no longer getting on by the time *The Big Sleep* was shot. His disapproval of her bond with Bogart left him silent. When the couple returned to the studio after their marriage, she says, everyone congratulated them, except Hawks. She even recalled 'someone on the picture stopping me on the lot one day and saying, "You know, you ought to call Howard. You ought to ask him for a date."' 'Why?' asked the foolish girl. '"Because he'd like it. He likes that – and he really likes you a lot. You could go over to his private office. Nobody would know about it." Boy, I was slow. It took some time before I realised what he was talking about.'

Hawks was never that slow, not where actresses were concerned, and not where his fantasies were alive. In *The Big Sleep*, for instance, the likelihood of any of several passing women being less than cute and willing is about as high as that of Gore Vidal splitting an infinitive. Howard Hawks was a womaniser. The available facts of his life make that clear – the tone of his movies raises flirtation to an art akin to rolling cigarettes or fashioning droll, drop-dead remarks.

So – and here some speculation is called for on the case – grant that Hawks felt his discovery, his type, slipping from his grasp as he came to do *The Big Sleep*. Isn't it possible, then, that he would turn to Carmen's role with fresh, wicked hopes? And doesn't that show on screen? Martha Vickers, his Carmen, was nine months younger than Bacall. A model previously, she had a few small roles in minor pictures. But Carmen was her chance. And Hawks took trouble with her: 'I made her sit around almost a day trying little things, taking a piece of hair and bringing it down and looking at it, you know. Because I didn't want her to be Stella Stevens or somebody like that. I wanted her to be a well-dressed little girl who just happened to be a nymphomaniac.'

Vickers is very good in the film, beautifully lit, as if someone had striven to get the shine of a flawed pearl, and allowed all variety of mannerisms – playing with her hair, sucking her thumb, and doing a sort of little girl's Mae West with wondering sighs. There was no way in 1945–6 that she could be as naked as the book had her. And in the movie not even her Chinese dress makes it unequivocal that she has been posing for pornographic pictures. But Hawks was good and randy enough to suggest nakedness. Did he try?

There is a fascinating letter from Raymond Chandler that hints at things. The letter is to Hamish Hamilton, his English publisher, and it is dated 30 May 1946 (three months before the movie's release). Chandler speaks very favourably of Bogart ('he has a sense of humor that contains that grating undertone of contempt') and Hawks (who has 'the gift of atmosphere and the requisite touch of hidden sadism'). But:

> *The Big Sleep* has had an unfortunate history. The girl who played the nymphy sister was so good she shattered Miss Bacall completely. So they cut the picture in such a way that all her best scenes were left out except one. The result made nonsense and Howard Hawks threatened to sue to restrain Warners from releasing the picture. After long arguments, as I hear it, he went back and did a lot of re-shooting.[5]

Though Chandler's is the only account that supports the idea of Vickers' excellence being deliberately reined in, there is something to the reshooting claim. Principal photograpy on *The Big Sleep* ended in January 1945. One of the original writers, Leigh Brackett, reported that there had been length problems while shooting – too many scenes – which Jules Furthman had tried to address:

> Furthman came into it considerably later, because Hawks had a great habit of shooting off the cuff. He had a fairly long script to begin with and he had no final script. He went into production with a 'temporary'. He liked to get a scene going and let it run. He eventually wound up with far too much story left than he had time to do on film. Jules came in and I think he was on it for about three weeks, and he rewrote it, shortening the latter part of the script.

Originally, the movie had had a 42-day schedule, yet it ended up going to 76 days on principal photography alone. The reasons for that were various: Bogart missed some days, apparently because of domestic disturbance – looking after Mayo, and romancing Bacall; even on set he was sometimes less than his best, maybe because of drinking; there was also the Hawksian habit of spending hours rewriting a scene, or reworking it with the actors; and there are hints that Bacall was less than effective. Even during principal photography there were days given over to retakes in order to get a better performance from her.

In other words, what ended up so happy and entertaining a picture emerged from Bogart's domestic nightmare, a torment in which Bacall must have suffered, too. One can see how the perfectionist Hawks might have been vexed that his 'Slim' had screwed it all up. So there might have been scenes that gave Carmen and Martha Vickers more room. Chandler even reports that Hawks considered an ending that involved Marlowe and Carmen. According to Chandler, Hawks was often dissatisfied with the script. In their subsequent talks they worked out this ending: Marlowe and Carmen go to Geiger's house at the end; by now, he knows that she is the killer; he also knows that the first person out of the door is going to get shot by Mars' men. This Marlowe wasn't sure how to act, so he tossed a coin:

> Before he tossed the coin he prayed out loud, in a sort of way. The gist of his prayer was that he, Marlowe, had done the best he knew

Tied up in Realito

> how and through no fault of his own was put in a position of making a decision God had no right to force him to make… If the coin came down heads, he would let the girl go. He tossed and it came down heads. The girl thought this was some kind of a game to hold her there for the police. She started to leave. At the last moment, as she had her hand on the doorknob, Marlowe weakened and started for her to stop her. She laughed in his face and pulled a gun on him. Then she opened the door an inch or two and you could see she was going to shoot and was thoroughly delighted with the situation. At that moment a burst of machine gun fire walked across the panel of the door and tore her to pieces.[6]

We know such considerations occurred, just because the same sort of fate awaits Eddie Mars – and the entire return to the Geiger house, with bullets through the door, is absent from the novel. Dramatically, perhaps, this is a better ending for Carmen, especially if she more thoroughly seduced and misled Marlowe.

All we know for certain is that, once shot, *The Big Sleep* waited an inordinate time: nearly twenty months elapsed between the close of principal photography and the film's release. In those days, as now, this was commonly a sign of lost confidence. On the one hand, Warners were intent on releasing any film that had war relevance – to beat the peace. Other pictures were put back. Equally, the delay could reflect cutting difficulties, and Hawks' threatened legal action.

Warner Brothers by then owned Bacall's contract and they wanted to build her as best they could. Right after *The Big Sleep* she was put into *The Confidential Agent*, from Graham Greene's novel (a wartime story), directed by Herman Shumlin, and co-starring Charles Boyer. That movie was actually released in 1945, and it flopped badly. Playing an aristocratic English woman, Bacall got terrible reviews of the kind that wondered if *To Have and Have Not* had been just a fluke. Or Hawks.

There was anxiety about her at the studio, not much lifted when the first version of *The Big Sleep* was released (some time around the spring and summer of 1945) for US forces in the Pacific theatre. In August 1945 the feeling at Warners was that 'Bacall about hundred times better in *Confidential* than she is in *Big Sleep*.'[7] By November, with domestic release still uncertain, Charlie Feldman begged Jack Warner to 'Give the girl [Bacall] at least three or four additional scenes with Bogart of the insolent and provocative nature that she had in *To Have and Have Not*.[8] Otherwise, he reckoned, she would get bad reviews again.

Warner responded. He said he had been thinking the very same thing. He gave the go-ahead for further shooting. What did that involve? The horse-racing scene, of course, but more. The April 1945 print recently discovered by the UCLA Film Archive reveals that the boudoir scene that includes Marlowe's 'Those are harsh words … especially when a man's walking out of your bedroom' was also added (instead of a lengthy chat between Marlowe and Norris). By January 1946 Warner was talking about 'two new sultry sequences' being added – and a thousand feet of film (over ten minutes) being taken out to make room and save the tempo. That, essentially, is the long-winded explanation scene. This new version was sneak previewed in February, and it was reckoned to be a hundred per cent improvement and a major protection for Bacall.

This doesn't mean that at an earlier stage other Carmen scenes weren't sacrificed. Martha Vickers got a contract at Warners out of it – and you can see why. To this day her scenes are edgy, nasty, and they involve a more credible woman than Vivian. She had some more pictures, but never anything anywhere near as impressive. Hawks had his version of what had happened to her; it fitted his foreboding verdict on any woman who forgot his lessons:

> Okay, she got her first salary check and went down and bought a lot of girly dresses with a lot of … little bows and ruffles and … she started playing a nice girl and they fired her after six months. And she came to me and said, 'What happened?' I said, 'You're just stupid. Why didn't you keep on playing that part?' 'Well, that was a nymphomaniac.' 'Look, it's only a nymphomaniac because I told you so. They liked you on the screen. And you did such a good job of it because you weren't trying to get sympathy or anything. You were a little bitch. Why didn't you keep doing that?'[9]

. . . .

Maybe Martha Vickers didn't understand the appeal of being 'a little bitch'. Is it something only men get? Maybe, without comprehension, she resisted the kind of lethal allure that Hawks had fashioned out of her hair, her thumb, her jittery narcissism and that pearly glow. I've never been convinced that Lauren Bacall grasped, liked or herself knew the thing that Hawks had made of her. She never worked for him again and – I'd venture to suggest – she was never as electric as she had been in those first two films she ever shot. There are plenty of actresses too solemn, too humourless, too adult, too mature, too responsible to just go on being 'the little bitch'. Bacall and Bogart got on with their real life, although there wasn't too much left: of being spouses, having children, being actors, being ordinary and conducting him to his death – all the situations and stories that are missing from the movies they made together. Yet they are now 'legendary', secure against fact; and maybe Hawks was on the mark in surmising that sometimes she had to keep on being 'Slim' if only so that the aging, ailing Bogart could stay 'Steve'. They named their own son Stephen, by the way.

Then consider this: Carmen never arouses Marlowe in the movie. It's not that he doesn't notice her: he sees her bare legs when she first comes downstairs at the Sternwood mansion; he smiles and teases her; he goes into his smart-talking routine. But she throws herself at him – quite literally – and he divines that there is some problem in Carmen, some impediment of sanity or maturity, that puts her off limits. For him to be

In Geiger's store in pursuit of 'a Ben Hur 1860' third edition, with the erratum on page 116

tempted by her would admit recesses of ordinary frailty in Marlowe that would horrify Hawks a good deal more than fucking a disturbed girl.

But this discretion is all the odder, or more mannered, if one reflects on the way the movie of *The Big Sleep* has variants on the little bitch like reel markers. Let me count them off, the girls who have scenes, moments, lines or glances, bees sniffing the honey that is Marlowe:

– there is the blonde in the library (not in the book), the one to whom Marlowe tosses the line that he sometimes collects blondes and bottles, too – the actress is Carole Douglas.

– There is Agnes Lozelle, in Geiger's shop, dumb on books but hip with grapefruit, and later the dreamgirl for Joe Brody and Harry Jones, both of whom (if you'll pardon the remark) are too small for her. Indeed, Marlowe has sized her up and knows how to whip her with words – he understands the bitch, and she looks at him with the bruised gratitude of someone who knows she's been understood. What ever happened to Sonia Darrin, who played Agnes?

– Then there's the girl at the Acme bookshop, the 20-year-old Dorothy Malone, who knows bibliography, has the instinct to close for the

Dorothy Malone, flirtatious as the Acme Bookstore proprietress

afternoon and who is, shall we say, obliging enough to slip off her glasses and put down her hair. 'We just did it,' reminisced Hawks, 'because the girl was so damn good-looking.'

– Don't forget the lady taxi driver (Joy Barlowe), who'll follow anything for Marlowe and gives him her card, making sure he knows when she's off duty. 'Wouldn't be bad,' he tells her, always the expert.

– Then there's the hatcheck girl (Lorraine Miller) and the cigarette girl (Shelby Payne) at Eddie Mars' place, who step on each other's lines trying to be first to talk to Marlowe.

– And finally there's Mona Mars (Peggy Knudsen) whom Marlowe admits to liking after he's goaded her into throwing her drink in his face.

Of those seven, the four sundries (librarian, taxi driver, hatcheck and cigarette) are not in the novel. While the Dorothy Malone role in the book concludes with her description of Geiger and Marlowe's estimate that she'd make a good cop. What follows in the movie is as exact, droll and outrageous as anything in Hawks. I've written about the scene elsewhere at length.[10] Let me just say now that with every passing year the scene becomes more problematic (and more a revelation of Hawks). On the one hand, the Malone character is presented as educated, intelligent and dedicated: she is working in a serious 'independent' bookstore, which today amounts to a kind of nunnery. She is also a very practical observer: her description of Geiger is professional. On the other hand, she is prepared to let the business of the store go to hell for … well, for what? For a drink and a couple of hours with a man she has never met before, and who acts like a poseur in a 'B' movie. (Bookstore row seemed to encourage playfulness in Bogart.)

What happens at the Acme? First of all, she meekly follows his notion of what an attractive woman should look like – she gives up her spectacles and what is apparently her preferred hairstyle. And then? I think we're meant to think that they have had sex – or were they just discussing rare editions and Marlowe's lingering attachment to the English language? So, OK, they were attracted and overwhelmed, and they did it. But then, as the story resumes, as Marlowe has to get back on the case, he throws her a 'Thanks, pal', and is on his way. And she does nothing to protest, to ask what now, what next, what about me? What did this mean? She has behaved like a placid whore, an available young bitch.

And Marlowe has sought no more. All of which may leave us wondering just what the 'marriage' between Marlowe and Vivian is going to be like. Maybe like the marriage of Hawks and Slim, when his union with a great-looking, intelligent woman never interfered with his feeling of having passing rights on anyone else. It's more than possible that those passing rights were actually exercised on some of the actresses who play our seven patient ladies.

The Acme scene is instructive in another way: it could be cut from the picture without any damage. And here, I think, we have reached something very important about both Hawks and *The Big Sleep*. The Acme scene, the horse-riding conversation and the screwball telephone call to police headquarters could all go without any loss in information or plot recognition. With this exception: without their pleasure, their fun (however queasy we may feel about it), we might be made more aware that we don't know what the hell the film is about. After all, audiences don't really appreciate confusion or their own difficulty in making sense of a film. To move only a few years away from *The Big Sleep*, there seems little doubt but that the narrative obscurity of *Citizen Kane* deterred viewers from 'following' or enjoying it.

One of the things of most historic interest about *The Big Sleep* is that it affected an indifference to narrative consequence that was startling. Hawks himself said often over the years that there had been a lesson in the film, about not needing to make sense, about having 'a good scene' or something that was 'fun', and carrying an audience along with you. Of course, we can see more clearly now that Hawks learned that lesson under some duress, or thanks to the second thoughts of the system. But it did work: no matter how poorly the first version of the picture previewed, on proper release the 'fatter', more digressive version grossed $3 million domestically – a major success. Fifteen years later, when I first saw the film, I was immediately taken with the exhilarating ease and pleasure. And I was not alone. That's how the film has become a classic, and why it still delights most audiences today.

There's a logic to that surgent illogicality, not to be missed. For there are other scenes that could go: Elisha Cook was never better than as Harry Jones, but we hardly need him or his clumsy way of getting us to Realito. Any decent constructionist could make that link without Harry – it might even help explain why Vivian is there. (Marlowe could follow her? Carmen could betray her sister? It's easy. And why are there no scenes of those sisters together?) Do we need Joe Brody or Agnes – yet are we prepared to lose that wonderfully shabby couple?

What I'm trying to suggest is that *The Big Sleep* – without fanfare or even self-awareness on Hawks' part – is one of the most formally radical pictures ever made in Hollywood. For it abandons story and genre as easily as one of its girls stepping out of her clothes, and says this is a movie about being a movie, about movie-ness. This is a kind of ongoing rehearsal or improvisation – very nicely done, mind you, there's need for untidiness (however open in design, Hawks was a precisionist in shooting). It's a picture about its own process, the fun of making fun. That's why it needed to be all on sets: not as a way of drawing down the claustrophobia, the trap, of Fritz Lang's world, but as a sign that the whole thing is a game, an artifice, a celebration of acting, dialogue (as opposed to talk) and fantasising. It is a dream about dreaming – maybe the best.

There's a prospect of decadence in that, I think – the way in which, as early as 1946, film had intuited the great gulf separating it from life. And it's part of the decadence that the Hawksian view of men and women is so headily adolescent. To say nothing of the loss in moral focus.

When the movie of *The Big Sleep* came out, Raymond Chandler was too impressed and excited to be critical. The film helped make him as an author. And Chandler was inexperienced enough, timid enough, to be captivated by the swaggering dream made by Hawks and Bogart. But as time passed, he was able to reflect. In 1949, Chandler was rather irked by an article John Houseman had written for *Vogue*, remarking on how Marlowe-like movies had little moral content. Chandler wrote to Houseman:

> I'm all for your demand that pictures, even tough pictures, and especially tough pictures, have a moral content. (Because *The Big Sleep* [the movie] had none I feel a little annoyed with you for not realizing that the book had a high moral content.) *Time* this week calls Philip Marlowe 'amoral'. This is pure nonsense. Assuming that his intelligence is as high as mine (it could hardly be higher), assuming his chances in life to promote his own interest are as numerous as they must be, why does he work for such a pittance? … It is the struggle of all fundamentally honest men to make a

decent living in a corrupt society. It is an impossible struggle; he can't win. He can be poor and bitter and take it out in wisecracks and casual amours, or he can be corrupt and amiable and rude like a Hollywood producer. Because the bitter fact is that outside of two or three technical professions which require long years of preparation, there is absolutely no way for a man of this age to acquire a decent affluence in life without to some degree corrupting himself, without accepting the cold, clear fact that success is always and everywhere a racket. [11]

That tells us so much about Chandler – the clash of naiveté and gloomy assertion, as well as the prickliness that hardly makes him easy company for Hollywood, or Hawks. There's much to be puzzled over, or disputed, especially the proposition that a writer cannot deliver a character who surpasses his own intelligence. But Chandler is right about Marlowe: the man *is* moral, and that primness is what leaves him hard to place or know as a literary creation. For Chandler wasn't good enough to explore the moral depth he claimed. In comparison, Harry Morgan in Hemingway's *To Have and Have Not* is a rough, battered but authentic moral being. It defines Hawks that he made Morgan and Marlowe brothers in the same witty, unreal isolation. But it's also a measure of Hawks' insight that he saw the comic wordsmith Chandler was never relaxed enough to liberate.

Equally, Chandler never managed a Philip Marlowe book in which Marlowe challenges the corruption of the city and the system, as opposed to the bizarre intricacies of a case that shows his debt to the classic English murder mystery. Chandler may have helped inspire Robert Towne, but he never grasped a scheme like that of *Chinatown* or delivered the tragedy of the private eye – funny, brave, resourceful, independent – who is overwhelmed by the system. And *Chinatown* has always stood as the vital link between a genre of fiction and the historic reality of Los Angeles, and America. It is a movie that believes in its story and its subject, and in the audience's need and capacity for a moral lesson.

Robert Altman's *The Long Goodbye* is aware of that gulf – and, of course, it was co-written by the Leigh Brackett who had helped Hawks. But Altman's Marlowe is a plausible outcast, a joke and a throwback to the real L.A. (it is a film full of actual locations and natural light), a man who should have a girl instead of a cat, and whose maleness is gently mocked by the naked ladies across the way (the little bitches turned into flower children). Elliott Gould was rather reviled as Marlowe (for *The Long Goodbye* came out in the heyday of the Bogie cult), but he is fine in the part, especially at conveying the sad, good-natured helplessness of Marlowe, and the mounting disquiet that needs to kill Terry Lennox (a rather Hawksian character).

But Chandler's Marlowe does not pay off finally until 1986 when he reappears, diseased, crippled outwardly and inwardly, somewhere between a premature corpse and an addicted fantasist, as Philip E. Marlow, the central figure in Dennis Potter's *The Singing Detective*. Here at last is a Marlowe who might rip the bed to pieces – if he had the strength.

. . . .

So where do I stand now on this most entertaining of films – and its rather sinister, but beguiling, director? I have tried to track the way in which fantasising, power plays and manoeuvre affected the making of the film. That gives cause for not taking Hawks at his own rugged self-estimate. He

Endgame: waiting for Eddie in Geiger's house

was a devious man, a liar, cruel at times, restricted in his savage intelligence, yet cocksure about it. He was a terrific movie-maker, yet does it really ease his enigma to set him up as an Artist? Maybe movie-makers are more complicated than that. There are things about *The Big Sleep* that ought to shame our pleasure – and at 55 I feel more confused about it than I could manage at 20.

Still, I hold to my love of Hawks, of his work, panache and movie-ness. I could have written another essay on *Bringing Up Baby*, for it is another version of the atmosphere of *The Big Sleep* in which fun, madness and order play their three-cushion dialogue games. (Think how easily a fuller version of the Carmen story could have been called *Bringing Up Baby*.)

The Big Sleep inaugurates a post-modern, camp, satirical view of movies being about other movies that extends to the New Wave and *Pulp Fiction*. In that sense, it breaks fresh ground while sensing the ultimate dead end of the form. And so I have to say, ruefully but with pleasure still, that *The Big Sleep* is both the most entertaining of films and a piece of shiny whimsy, untrue to life in so many important ways. After a hundred years of film, intelligent commentary seems to be left with that embarrassing conclusion.

NOTES

· ·

1 *Hawks on Hawks*, ed. Joseph McBride
(Berkeley, CA: University of California Press,
1982), p. 96.

2 Lauren Bacall, *By Myself* (New York:
Knopf, 1979), p. 91.

3 Louise Brooks, *Lulu in Hollywood* (New
York: Knopf), p. 66.

4 *Hawks on Hawks*, p. 102.

5 Chandler to Hamish Hamilton, 30 May
1946, in *Selected Letters of Raymond Chandler*,
ed. Frank MacShane (New York: Columbia
University Press, 1981), p. 76.

6 Ibid.

7 Jack Warner to Ben Kalmenson, 23 August
1945, in Rudy Behlmer (ed.), *Inside Warner
Brothers* (New York: Simon & Schuster,
1985), pp. 248–9.

8 Charles Feldman to Jack Warner, 16
November 1945, ibid., p. 248.

9 Quoted in John Kobal, *People Will Talk*
(New York: Knopf, 1985), p. 498.

10 David Thomson, 'At the Acme Book
Shop', *Sight & Sound*, Spring 1981.

11 Chandler to John Houseman, circa
October 1949, in *Selected Letters of Raymond
Chandler*, p. 197.

CREDITS

. . . .

The Big Sleep

USA
1946
US copyright date
31 August 1946
US release
31 August 1946
US distributor
Warner Bros. Pictures
UK tradeshow
3 October 1946
UK release
21 October 1946
UK distributor
Warner Brothers Pictures
Production company
Warner Bros Pictures, Inc.
A Howard Hawks
Production
Executive producer
Jack L. Warner
Director
Howard Hawks
Assistant directors
Chuck Hansen, Robert
Vreeland
Screenplay
William Faulkner, Leigh
Brackett, Jules Furthman,
based on the novel by
Raymond Chandler
**Photography
(black and white)**
Sid Hickox
Music
Max Steiner
Music director
Leo F. Forbstein
**Orchestral
arrangements**
Simon Bucharoff
Song
'Her tears flowed like wine'
Editor
Christian Nyby
Art director
Carl Jules Weyl
Set decorator
Fred M. MacLean

Wardrobe
Leah Rhodes
Make-up artist
Perc Westmore
Special effects
E. Roy Davidson
(director),
Warren E. Lynch, William
McGann, Robert Burks
Sound
Robert B. Lee
114 minutes

Humphrey Bogart
Philip Marlowe
Lauren Bacall
Vivian Rutledge
John Ridgely
Eddie Mars
Martha Vickers
Carmen Sternwood
Dorothy Malone
*Acme Bookstore
proprietress*
Peggy Knudsen
Mona Mars
Regis Toomey
Bernie Ohls
Charles Waldron
General Sternwood
Charles D. Brown
Norris, the butler
Robert Steele
Canino
Elisha Cook, Jr.
Harry Jones
Louis Jean Heydt
Joe Brody
Carole Douglas
Librarian
Sonia Darrin
Agnes
Forbes Murray
Furtive man at Geiger's
Tom Rafferty
Carol Lundgren
Theodore Von Eltz
Arthur Gwynn Geiger

Emmett Vogan
Ed, deputy sheriff
Joseph Crehan
Medical examiner
Joy Barlowe
Taxi driver
Ben Welden
Pete
Tom Fadden
Sidney
Lorraine Miller
Hatcheck girl
Shelby Payne
Cigarette girl
Jack Chefe
Croupier
Kenneth Gibson
Man at roulette table
**Paul Webber,
Jack Perry,
Wally Walker**
Mars' henchmen
**Janis Chandler,
Deannie Bert**
Waitresses
Trevor Bardette
Art Huck
Pete Kooy
Motorcycle cop

**Cut from
1946 release print:
Dan Wallace**
Owen Taylor
Thomas Jackson
District Attorney Wilde
James Flavin
Captain Cronjager

Credits checked by
Markku Salmi.

The print of *The Big Sleep*
in the National Film and
Television Archive was
aquired specially for the 360
Classic Feature Films
project from United
International Pictures (UK).

A note on casting

The Hawks archive at
Brigham Young University
includes a casting list (dated
13 September 1944) from
Hawks himself. This offers
some intriguing alternatives
to the eventual cast. For
instance, the role of General
Sternwood was once meant
for H.B. Warner or Harry
Davenport. Eve Amber is
mentioned for Agnes; Dan

Duryea (who had been in
Ball of Fire) for Joe Brody.
Beside the role of Eddie Mars
there were two names – Paul
Stewart and John Ireland;
Ireland was also suggested for
the role of Canino. Joan
Loring was the initial thought
for Carmen, while the
'bookstore girl' had three
possibles, including 'Dorothy
Maloney' (Malone's real
name). Pat Clark was cast as

Mona Mars, and she actually
shot scenes. But in the second
round of shooting, those
scenes were redone, with
Peggy Knudsen in the role.

Some cast lists still include
the character of 'Captain
Cronjager', played by James
Flavin. This role was part of
the 'explanation' sequence
deleted before proper release.

BIBLIOGRAPHY

· ·

Lauren Bacall, *By Myself* (New York: Knopf, 1979).

Rudy Behlmer (ed.), *Inside Warner Bros (1935–51)* (New York: Viking, 1985).

Peter Bogdanovich, *The Cinema of Howard Hawks* (New York: Museum of Modern Art, 1962).

Louise Brooks, 'Humphrey and Bogey', in *Lulu in Hollywood* (New York: Knopf, 1982).

Leigh Brackett, 'A Comment on the Hawksian Woman', *Take One*, July–August 1971.

Raymond Chandler, *The Big Sleep* (New York: Knopf, 1939).

William Faulkner, Leigh Brackett and Jules Furthman, *The Big Sleep* (screenplay) in *Film Scripts One*, ed. George P. Garrett, O. B. Hardison Jr and Jane R. Gelfman (New York: Appleton-Century-Crofts, 1971).

Aljean Harmetz, *Round Up the Usual Suspects* (New York: Hyperion,1992).

Brooke Hayward, *Haywire* (New York: Knopf, 1977).

Ernest Hemingway, *To Have and Have Not* (New York: Scribners, 1937).

Dorris Johnson and Ellen Leventhal (eds.), *The Letters of Nunnally Johnson* (New York: Knopf, 1981).

Slim Keith, with Annette Tapert, *Slim* (New York: Simon & Schuster, 1990).

John Kobal, *People Will Talk* (New York: Knopf, 1985).

Gavin Lambert, *Norma Shearer: A Biography* (New York: Knopf, 1990).

Joseph McBride, *Hawks on Hawks* (Berkeley, CA: University of California Press, 1982).

Patrick McGilligan (ed.), interview with Leigh Brackett, *Backstory 2* (Berkeley, CA: University of California Press, 1991).

Frank MacShane, *The Life of Raymond Chandler* (New York: Dutton, 1976).

– (ed.), *Selected Letters of Raymond Chandler* (New York: Columbia University Press, 1981).

Gerald Mast, *Howard Hawks: Storyteller* (New York: Oxford University Press, 1982).

Movie, December 1962.

Thomas Schatz, *The Genius of the System* (New York: Pantheon, 1988).

Richard Schickel, *The Men Who Made the Movies* (New York: Atheneum, 1975).

– *Double Indemnity* (London: British Film Institute, 1992).

David Thomson, 'At the Acme Book Shop', *Sight & Sound*, Spring 1981.

Robert Towne, *Chinatown* (Santa Barbara, CA: Neville, 1983).

Peter Wollen, *Signs and Meaning in the Cinema* (London: Secker & Warburg, British Film Institute, 1969).

Robin Wood, *Howard Hawks* (London: Secker & Warburg, British Film Institute, 1968.

ALSO PUBLISHED

. . . .

If you would like further
information about future
BFI Film Classics or
about other books on
film, media and popular
culture from BFI
Publishing, please write
to:

BFI Film Classics
British Film Institute
21 Stephen Street
London
W1P 2LN

BFI FILM

CLASSICS

THE BIG HEAT

....

Colin McArthur

"Film Classics - *one of the best ideas BFI Publishing has had*"
SUNDAY TIMES

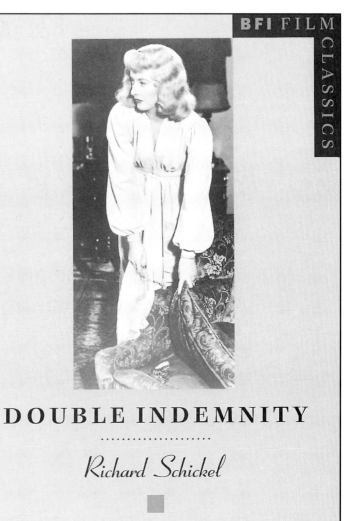

BFI FILM

CLASSICS

DOUBLE INDEMNITY

....

Richard Schickel

"*A fine account of Billy Wilder's struggle to adapt
James M. Cain's hard-boiled novel for the screen*"
TIME OUT

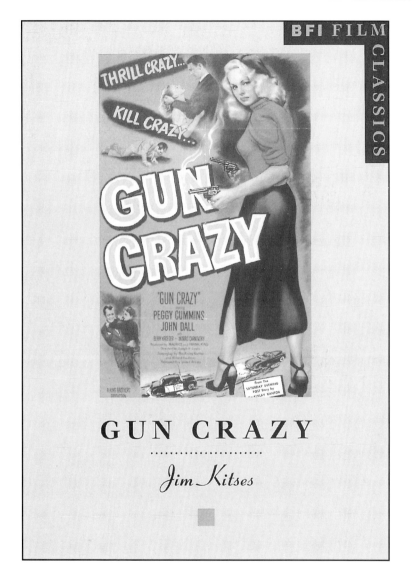

BFI FILM CLASSICS

GUN CRAZY

....

Jim Kitses

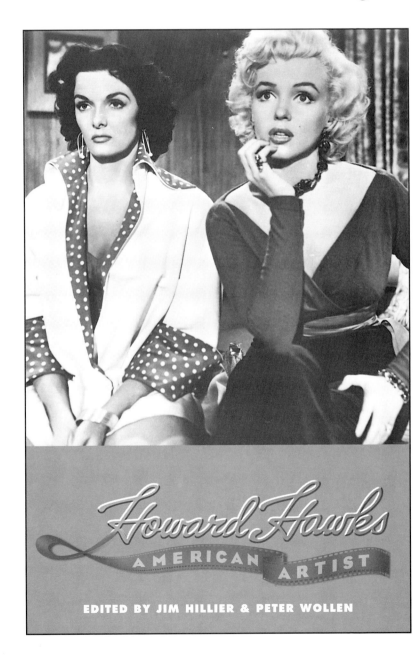

Howard Hawks
AMERICAN ARTIST

EDITED BY JIM HILLIER & PETER WOLLEN